SCAPEGOAT

―――――――――

The Next Poems

by

T.K. Lee

SCAPEGOAT
Copyright © 2022 T.K. LEE
All Rights Reserved.
Published by Unsolicited Press.
Printed in the United States of America.
First Edition.

No part of this book may be used or reproduced in any manner whatsoever without written permission except in the case of brief quotations embodied in critical articles or reviews.

Attention schools and businesses: copies are available through Ingram. Special sales can be made by emailing sales@unsolicitedpress.com

Unsolicited Press
Portland, Oregon
www.unsolicitedpress.com
info@unsolicitedpress.com
619-354-8005

Cover Design: Kathryn Gerhardt
Image Provided by Danielle Bruce
Editor: S.R. Stewart

ISBN: 978-1-956692-29-7

In this collection, the following poems have been previously published, anthologized, and/or awarded: "Hospitality" (in the inaugural edition of *Equinox*, 2021); "Sapelo" (*Open: Journal of Arts and Letters*, 2019); "Neck and Neck," (Clarendon House Publishing, UK, 2019); "Native," (quarterfinalist for the Pangaea Prize, 2018; published as a stand-alone poem through *Parliament Literary Journal*, 2021); and lastly, the following three poems, "Break(fast)," along with "Postmodern Realism," and "Native" (published yet again, as a stand-alone poem) have been anthologized through Sunday Mornings at the River Poetry Press (UK) for international distribution.

"I hate and I love.
And if you ask me how,
I do not know:
I only feel it, and
I am
torn in two."

Catullus

TABLE OF CONTENTS

PROLOGUE
HOSPITALITY — 11

NURTURE
NECK AND NECK — 15
IMITATIO — 16
OLD DOGS — 18
THE ACCIDENT OF A CIVILIZED MAN — 27
NATIVE — 35

NATURE
FULL LOVE — 49
TRESPASS — 59
POSTMODERN REALISM — 61
THE ONE WITH THE DAISIES — 62
BREAK(FAST) — 68
ALTRUISM — 69
SCAPEGOAT — 70

EPILOGUE
SAPELO — 89

PROLOGUE

*Come back. Even as a shadow.
Even as a dream.*

—EURIPEDES

HOSPITALITY

There are two of them. Let's say: It's a father and a son. (It isn't. It is an uncle and his
nephew).
76 to 42.
Such a distance
hangs on every word. Here are two men thrown a life of never quite
    knowing his place,
which chair at the table to sit in, what to do at night with the curtains.
These men, though, appreciate that distance is measure not fate. That it is it not a game
of counting years leaving to years left.   ///   In the back right
corner, at the window in the hall, facing what's left of the silo, the
    carpet, loose, came
up, on the back of a heel, felled the uncle to his knees, in the broad
    daylight.   ///

Their dog and pony of *It's not the old that want to leave the young*, a
    point less
dynamic in the bright of new worry: What would find its way back to
    the middle.

What found its way back was a mess.

The house, a curiosity now more than a comfort. The nephew now,
    little
        by   little,

stoops his shoulders, crying uncle, aware at how often they make the
    same faces
about the same things.   They have come to make nothing
but faces, in fact.   It is this recognition that places each
man unapologetically beside what he <u>knew</u> of loving.
Besides, what he <u>knows</u> of
loving now's schedul**ed** appointments, schedul**ing** appointments, a
    landline in the waiting room,
a nurse's name, another nurse's name, another nurse's name, another—
    enough to keep each man make-believing that soon:

They'll be back to *the coast, this summer? Come fall,* back to *the*
    mountains, camera in hand:
Collect a leaf as it turns **when we go.**
Consider the grains of sand **when we go.**

The Necessary Lie of a photo is that it'll be the good one. A boast of leaf
    and mountain,
a brag of coast and sand. They never got a good one though. ///
The ones they do have are all the same: An ~~older~~ olding man,
    a younger man
half a smile on each as they prostate in Meridian, heart to Jackson, lung
    at Tupelo

These two, like father, like son, in a house made of corners. They've
    been
        waiting their turn to speak
  like this since it was 36 to 3.

NURTURE

*If it's not Here,
that means it's out There*
—WINNIE THE POOH

NECK AND NECK

I would not be like you
a giant, afraid of being a giant, concerned with
the common business of small talk because it isn't
too big, too loud, too much in the way. I won't be

a giant afraid of being a giant. Concerned with
when to stand, to sit, to speak, to think. *What's worse*:
Too big? Too loud? Too much in the way? (I won't be).
No giant is ever the footnote instead of the story.

When to stand, to sit, to speak, to think! *What's worse?*
The giant you never know is there or the one you see but can't catch?
(No giant is ever the footnote instead of the story).
I stay bothered by how much I worried that

the giant you never know is there or the one you see but can't catch
stood beside you, already full-seen and caught—a fool.
I stay bothered by how much I worried that
I would not be like you.

IMITATIO[1] [2]

1.
But of indifference, ~~wasn't he~~ no? He was **(he was!)** still learning,
Brueghel, painting his *Fall of Icarus*, wanting for the first time
to suffer without some fool-woman burning
this or that dinner or some fool-man returning home with traffic, late
again for this dinner for that leftover dinner for something like dinner.
   Until he began to notice the children—sprung forth wholly made
swollen with such indifference—at how capably they could climb out of
cribs, disturbing plate and cup, of fleshy cheek and lip, trying to remind
their jabberjaw parents how easy it is to forget:
If what goes up **must** come down, then falling isn't failing. It's
        another way of flying

2.
You're thinking: Icarus chose to drown, a purposeful glut of wax and
        wing; or better yet,
you're thinking: Brueghel should've done more about skinned knees,
        less about the sinner.

---

[1] For W.H. Auden, in response to his poem, "Musee does Beaux Arts," an ekphrastic reply to Brueghel's *Landscape with the Fall of Icarus.*

2 Imitatio is the study and conspicuous deployment of features recognizably characteristic of a canonical author's style or content, so as to define one's own generic affiliation.

3.
Brueghel's different. Bothered his brush can't pull **but** a glance from
	the budding, callow head
of the plough man—an offish man ignorant to his own age who'd rather
	keep to his work instead
as if he can persuade Brueghel that for a grown man to stay the course,
	he
	has to let
Icaruses sop into gobs of boiled feathers, each a lesson learned and
	every one in front of his own face!
 The plough man though (and we're meant to be the plough man, to
  this extent)
will come to realize he's (read: we're) left to be the only witness…
  without consent
		without any dinner at all, and without regret
			for not caring in the first place.

OLD DOGS[3]

1.
You were ordinary,
the way you'd stand—
        dull, erect   alone.
Punished Apostle of
the Pedestrian
              in the hot
              of the day—

                        you fashioned
                        a crowd of two
                        your shadow and you

                        muttering, wondering
                        out loud
                        at the riddle
                        of a cracking sidewalk—

when you moved,
you shook enough earth to look busy—
        one eye
        staring
        ahead /
        the other eye

---

[3] For Randall Jarrell

    staying
    closed/
    you kept yourself
    in circles.

    Your mother said
        that's why

        you quit (your mother said

you'd *joked*
about quitting before
but *on a Thursday*)

2.

        —arms akimbo
        legs scattershot
        against that Prussian beard

you lay there
deaf to the hanging-on world
    while in the street beside you
    every other church-child who
had long been warned not to
listen *listened*

the thrust of your loud-quiet
        punch-drunk prophecy

    ran stray
            (*church-children have such sticky lobes*)
in the Jitney Jungle
        like the natives
        like the loafs
            with their baited bread
            which they use
            like a threat like a lure
            to pinch off and throw
            at the local fish

3.
an insult, too,
how unnoticed you went, previously,
even with
how near you stood, closely walked
        (right next to real-on-the-earth people
        tied in place to their tugged-at ears)

a real shame
        you   ~~couldn't~~   ~~didn't~~   **wouldn't** use both eyes
        so you could full-see
        they couldn't half-hear
        how much you preferred that

4.
Can't do a thing about it now,
your mother said.

Can't
go back / we can't
do backwards. *It's ridiculous!*

If we went backwards,
he'd still never see,
he wouldn't hear
that blame car coming up behind—don't be absurd.
        (You would have laughed like the rest of us
        though I doubt you'd have been first).

5.
Every single person stared
at you
        lying
        there like you were.
        Some saw a man, suffered gladly.

I saw a mountain
                stopped body
                heaped onto itself
                rubbled like fallen rock.
A woman who meant well—with a small red-faced kid at-knee—
on her brisk-curt-quick way to the zoo—

with what passed as a glance to spare
hollered out loud to everyone there
that it *couldn't be you.*

                              To everyone she passed by too.
                              She didn't stop; she kept on walking.

                              Like she was someone we all knew

I would have leaned in, at least, to make sure.
Would've done a close read
of your forehead

        for the kept zeal
        in that constant crease
        of your telltale brow.
                That's how
                I'd have done it to make sure.

6.
I forget
why you went out
into the street

(I wasn't there).

                    They thought it best to say you were "distracted by ____."
                            A last Elavil (with its clumsy pill bottle).

							A stub of a cigarette (likely still lit).

											Okay, maybe.
					Or maybe
					it was
some younger man, too familiar with a crowd,

born out
		already long in the arm as you,
		same grip on a word
		except what you made loud
											he didn't

(so they all took him to be nicer—
											it happens).

Did he call
to you/ did he
		use your full-given
				Jesus-Christer.

											No
					no,
						no		no. You being you,
										It wasn't a Him.
										It was a Her.
										It was some woman
		mary-magdalen-ing the sidewalk
		busking little more than noise.

Those
                at gawk
around her didn't care who
you were anyhow
                anymore than she did.
She swore her baby boy was under
        your rubbled brow,
              in near repose
              still dead
              still being

                                      (the irony)
                          washed out of the turret
        still holding
                the hose.

If she called you a name at all (God knows)
    that's it, is it?, that
            age pulls you
            further away
from your Name,
until you're no longer familiar
        can't even tell if you're a person, a place, a *thing*.

        That's a particular shame
        since a name
        is all three.

7.
There was never going to be
anyone who could
        tell you that
        a car was coming
        to remind you to
        look both ways
                Of course, you can't keep a name
                you no longer have.

8.
    Some say
    you did
    hear that car
        before you crossed
        ~~the Styx~~   the street
        before you stepped
                off
    the cracked sidewalk
    right out in front of that car.
        He probably did hear that car coming! Some say
        that you did it on purpose.
        A few say that ~~probably~~ what it was,
                it was ~~an accident~~.

9.
    I say: Running away is hard work,

            especially
        when you lose sight
          of what your name looks like
            especially
        when you forget how
           people, places, and things sound,
            especially
        when you can't tell the difference
           between

hard ground
and grass growing green
enough

to let you know
where

            or even when
          the city comes   to   an   end.

THE ACCIDENT OF A CIVILIZED MAN

1.
he monks along
a kitchen window
      devoted to
      making a habit
of curtains drawn

of certain dishes
      in the same
      place/half
           of the sink

2.
a modern day
      spent
      at rake
in hand while

    the same   buzzard pulls at
    the same   deer neck
                  plated in a ditch
                  wild with sweet
    william cloistered
    in an unmade bed

St. Augustine
leans too near
    the rabbit tobacco
        rogues
    in August heat

    broken-in beneath
the old gospel
of a dirt road
/
a paved over
liturgy
    too good for the buzzard
    too late for the deer

3.
homegrown mad
handmade old
    the mouth a shadow now
    a finished saint
teasing what grace is
found left behind
in a tongue
born-again and fat
    from another day's bread
        of a ripe old pilgrim
        tithing his last yeast
            as he needs,

                sure of each hour
                his knees
                      kept bent
beside the calla lillies
which are beside the begonias
which are where the daisies were
     there
beside where the impatiens used to be
in the well-worn-out dirt
turned up
like the meager pine
toward Beulah Land

        "Progress is   the only shrine"
                      to understand

                      you
                      took

  to the world
  a cultivated anger:

(Dawn has always been
yoked to dusk)
                but

    you
    were not
    the burden /

        you remarked,
        No

    but
    every single one of my days
    begins
the way it ends—
      flocked
      in dark

4.
each night
    found you
over the kitchen
sink   the same teaspoon to chapped lip
            head against glass
hair, a white crust
(perhaps your magic
trick was to hide
    an old goat
    in a crop
    of biscuits)

        my eye is sharp
        enough
        now
I could cut
    the grass

    through the kitchen window
    if I wanted to

    if you wanted me

      to

5.
the way you taught me
to

  see   stubborn

as magic
made
manifest

         with doubt
         as her conjure

6.
(the regret of)
electrical tape handles

      the push mower
      just fine

(the grief of) using
a bobby pin learns
    the weight of shoulders
    on a clothes-line

in the way of our worship we work
a well-known
Call & Response

    Me : <u>We need a new mower—</u>
    You : *The yard don't know the difference.*

    Me : <u>We need a new dryer—</u>
    You : *The clothes don't know the difference.*

two sides
of a
crackerjack
    coin peeled
by your callous
world-of-worn
    fingers

        you kept one side and that was fair
        except
        the other side
        you also kept:
            a debt paid

    for the forty years
      of milk
that have soured the front yard,
        (my wilderness)

    for the forty more
      of honey
that have tarred the flat tire
        swing (my pillar of fire)

7.
I see
that now

      how wise
      you were
      to
            take that
            teaspoon full of
            home-made poison

            to throw right
            back up / a
            habit

of the sink
after dinner
            with one eye searching me :

Every season has its sinner.

I see
        now
        that
        what's forgotten,
            <u>*isn't*</u>;
          it has

        only become
                familiar

NATIVE[4]

Sylvia,
my birthday was Sunday.

42.
I needed—well,
      I *wanted* so I'd ordered—
a new jacket, nothing else.
I didn't want another thing
not really. A simple, inexpensive coat, really. I didn't want a
heavy coat, either, a jacket
lined like the trench
you preferred. A long shoulder, a high collar.
I'd do fine with a lighter
sleeve, a tender mercy of cloth,
a thick enough thread
against the little rain that lies
in wait for the small walks
      I say I'll take at least
to where the foothills start
          I told the UPS man

---

[4] For Sylvia Plath

My asthma keeps me pebble-level.
No mountains for me
                      I told him.
                          I say he listened
                  but I have also told a lie already
                      because

Sylvia,

I wanted

a day at the zoo too. I wanted a new jacket

and a day at the zoo. So,

    I went to the zoo

in my new jacket, Sylvia.

                  If you could've seen me!

    At how

I walked to the car

waterproofed,

slick-creased,

wicked

against a coming sweat—

    at how

I walked up to purchase a day-pass

slick as water

creased proof

in a dusty gray, deep-threaded pattern.

I felt attractive in that
color despite
what you said
about me in that color.
                      (*It's not a color*,
you said, *You know what looks good
in that color? Nothing*, you said,
which means, I suppose,
I'm nothing to look at— I know
                      that's not what you meant).

I went
to the bathroom
with the good mirror
to take a picture of myself
on the iPhone.

                I wasn't alone
                in the bathroom.
A fish was there
in the mirror, in the bathroom
mirror. It was

                your fish, Sylvia:
                Same side-silver streak, same
                wide, stupid mouth, open, same
                fat, stilled by bloat. Same dead

left eye, right eye missing.

      (You named him
Gilbert—you said to keep that
to myself, I know). I snapped

a picture of him too

on the iPhone. (I made the same face
as he did, standing there
          staring—I
brushed my teeth, too hard as usual,
red spittle on the faucet—
        this is how I tell the truth—
asked him how he'd been).
          Then,
I snapped the picture.
            Then,
    I went to the zoo
in my birthday jacket.

I stood in line for a ticket
on the train that circles
the zoo?
(It was a short line

dragged along
by
that same horrible no-respecter-of-persons minute
as is every minute when
you wait
for what everybody else has.

    The train came
finally,
and I had my doubts)

        There was a young girl put
           beside me, her mother the row in front—
the sun, even in December, Sylvia, was hot.
I didn't even need a jacket with a light sleeve—
        the rain had even stopped.
This young girl. Her arms, her box
of a head, a baked apple.
    She didn't speak to me. Children shouldn't speak.
    Her mother spoke to me.
    Mothers speak to everybody.

We sat there, a zoo-family, among the
thousand-felt-like other children with mothers
(without fathers?) who had guts of noise and

who, dirty fingers all, pointed as
round and round and round we went!,

yelling out animal names, as

we choo-chooed

beside each exhibit: Alligators!!, Flamingoes!, Monkeys!!,
Lion!

> Lio<u>n</u>? Yes.
> Lion.

Just the one, Sylvia,

in a stated cage beneath

the wooden bridge—the train idled

for people to get off

> for people picturing—
> to give them room to air their mock-surprise
> of finding just the one

lion, Sylvia.

His wife died last month, the conductor hollered
through the grinning static of his microphone.

> *Her name was Loo-Loo*, the conductor hollered,
> his fingers pinching the cord,

my zoo-wife pretended at a tear,
squeezed our zoo-daughter — who was cooked
from the sun, remember? — she cried
at being squeezed after
being cooked by the sun.

And now he can't roar…ever since the conductor hollered.
All the zoo-families ogling, rubbering their necks with
more genuine surprise of a lion
that stopped roaring.
    Laid out, as he was,
on the top of a concrete slab, jaws open,
all-capital-letters-like.

The very idea of a lion who couldn't roar, the conductor hollered,
Or <u>wouldn't</u>.
    Some child yelled, "Look, he's about to roar!"
He was yawning.

    He does that a lot, the conductor hollered.

Maybe that's why
he won't roar
anymore, Sylvia.

Maybe his jaws have grown
a permanent yawn.

    Same child yelled, "What if it's a new kind of roar we can't hear!?
        The conductor hollered,
        Well, he'd catch you for sure then!

Since I found myself
at the rail of the bridge,
I showed him the photo
of Gilbert—
don't worry, I didn't tell him Gilbert's name—
      he wasn't even
interested, he looked away from me.

    So I yelled—you know I never yell—
"Oh, what?!, you too good
to look at a picture
of a dead fish,
you dumb lion!"

    I laughed at myself. Everyone else seemed bothered by that.
    The conductor winked
        at a nearby family, "All aboard!"

                    I went

to place the iPhone back into

a new gray jacket pocket of its own

when I realized it was the photo of myself
I'd shown

him, Sylvia!

Not of the fish

which made the rain

       we found— so quick! —ourselves

standing in

      — plop plop! —

              somehow

more urgent, all front-page, if risible and

Sylvia,

if I'm being honest,

as rude

as you used to be,

the more necessary

you decided to become.

          I got back on the train.
          A row to myself now.
          I wanted to

sit very still. I was upset—
wet when I shouldn't be—
                I didn't even look up to see
the elephants, which you know
is my favorite animal.
                Sylvia.
                No,
I kept my hands in my pockets,
that's a thing I like to do now,
kept my elbows at my side. I opened
and closed my mouth several times
to take hold of my best breath.
                I held a few in,
pretended I was a fishing pole,
or a casserole dish, or a night light,
something quiet so I wouldn't bite
the ears off everyone on that train
                pretended even
there were no such things
as elephants or new jackets or zoos
or baked apples or daughters or trains
or fish or Sundays
                or widowed lions.
                or no,
                I'm sorry….lio*n*.

There's just the one, Sylvia.

There's just the one
lion.

NATURE

Yes is a world
and in this world of
yes [...] live all worlds.
—E.E. CUMMINGS

FULL LOVE

A text at
    9:00PM

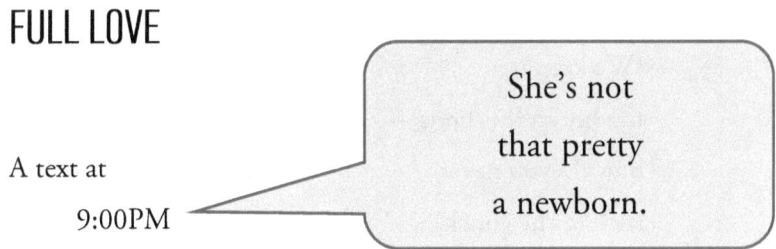

She's not that pretty a newborn.

Blanket commentary.
And it's always true,
    for every baby,
        isn't it?

(A picture followed, 9:05).

        See, I wasn't lying.

        (which only proved you know how to).

That picture.
I laughed.   Hard
                    enough

I had to pee.
I had to peel
myself away from
the couch.

(We keep it

too hot in this house—

how do you never

stick to the couch).

        I tried to make up a joke that would end with

        "*well, at least it's nice to be wanted*"…but I quit

        halfway into it because I'm no good at jokes.

                I laugh in the wrong places.

                I punch the wrong lines.

    I made
another drink while I was up. Then,
     while I was up,

    I made another drink.
all the while
knowing the sink was full of every other glass, left unwashed
so I picked one up
rinsed it out
pretended it was brand new.

    I wanted ice
all the while
knowing that the ice maker was still broken
so I told myself I still didn't need any ice
pretended there had never been any ice too.

    I wanted aspirin, Tylenol, ibuprofen.
all the while
knowing there was no aspirin, Tylenol, ibuprofen
so I decided to have a headache
because that was what I had to do.

    I leaned against the kitchen island,
    and wondered at the number

of other ugly babies

I had ever

seen.

    I   was surprised

        at how many

        I came up with.

        It was <u>*all*</u> of them—

        which is what I'd thought—

I tried to think next
of the *ugliest*,

    squatting on
    the floor of the pantry
    hungry
        (for a house
        brined in Home).
        What was *ugliest* anyway, really.
        I looked up—

I was at the refrigerator somehow—
only to realize — like that!—
I was late for work now.

Late for work *again,* I should say—

(**I** hate that

I depend

on you)   to frustrate

       me into being

necessary: unlike
- the dog, in-medias-res whine, for you, room to room, on the hour/
- the mail, I didn't get yesterday, or today, which will become tomorrow's mail/
- the clothes, that I put in the washer, that I will wait too late to put in the dryer/

(the line between **help** and **help<u>less</u>** has always been there if you know how to spell)

  which is why
        I am not surprised
when I find you ate the last
of the chicken fried rice.
        I am surprised
I didn't starve to death.
        I am not surprised
when I find you used the last
of the almond creamer in your coffee for the two-hour drive down.

      I am surprised
I didn't die of thirst.
      I am not surprised
when you aren't in the orange swivel
playing Words
with Friends
by yourself
in the room
we don't sit in without good company

(After all, you're out of town)
                                            but
      I am surprised
      it took a moment
      for me to realize why
                      I can't recognize
                      the house anymore—
which is why
I might as well be
the knock at the door.
I might as well be
the good company kept waiting
I might as well be
the room we don't sit in.

I don't like
> being lonely. I like
> being   .
> > > > alone.

You used to know
> the difference.

Another text
> at 11:00.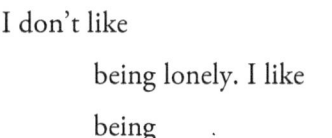

Some things never change! I always lose and Sorry.

> > > > Before I could reply

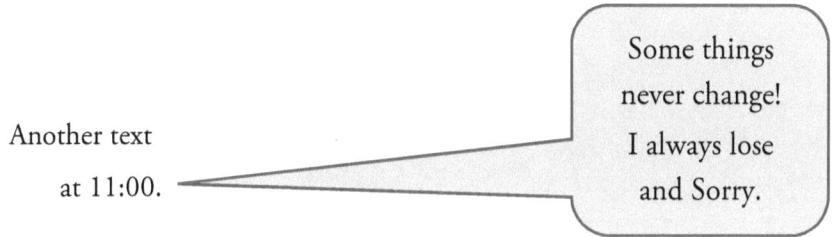

AT. Sorry! Auto-correct. I lost AT Sorry. My sister and her board games!

Another text
> at 11:03

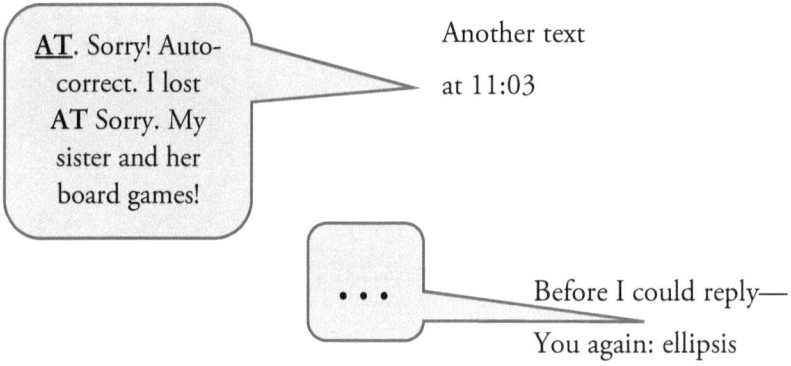

> > > Before I could reply—
> > > You again: ellipsis

> > > I hold a wasted breath.

She's not going to breastfeed. at 11:07.

Then at 11:08.

I'm coming home Thursday, not Friday.

11:09

11:10

11:11

11:12
11:13

you said nothing

and nothing again at 11:14.

I was giving up and getting up when
                    at 11:15
there came your familiar ping ping ping

the iPhone (as lit as I was) and me
at the end of a string
you forgot you'd tied to your finger.

I hadn't seen
        the cats
        in two days
                I was reading
        that biography
        on Walter Anderson
        this morning. He tried to
        tie himself to a hurricane—
        (I didn't even wonder at why
        he would do that. So, I
        stopped reading the book
        as a courtesy)
now
    Thursday seems as far away as you do

                when
                here

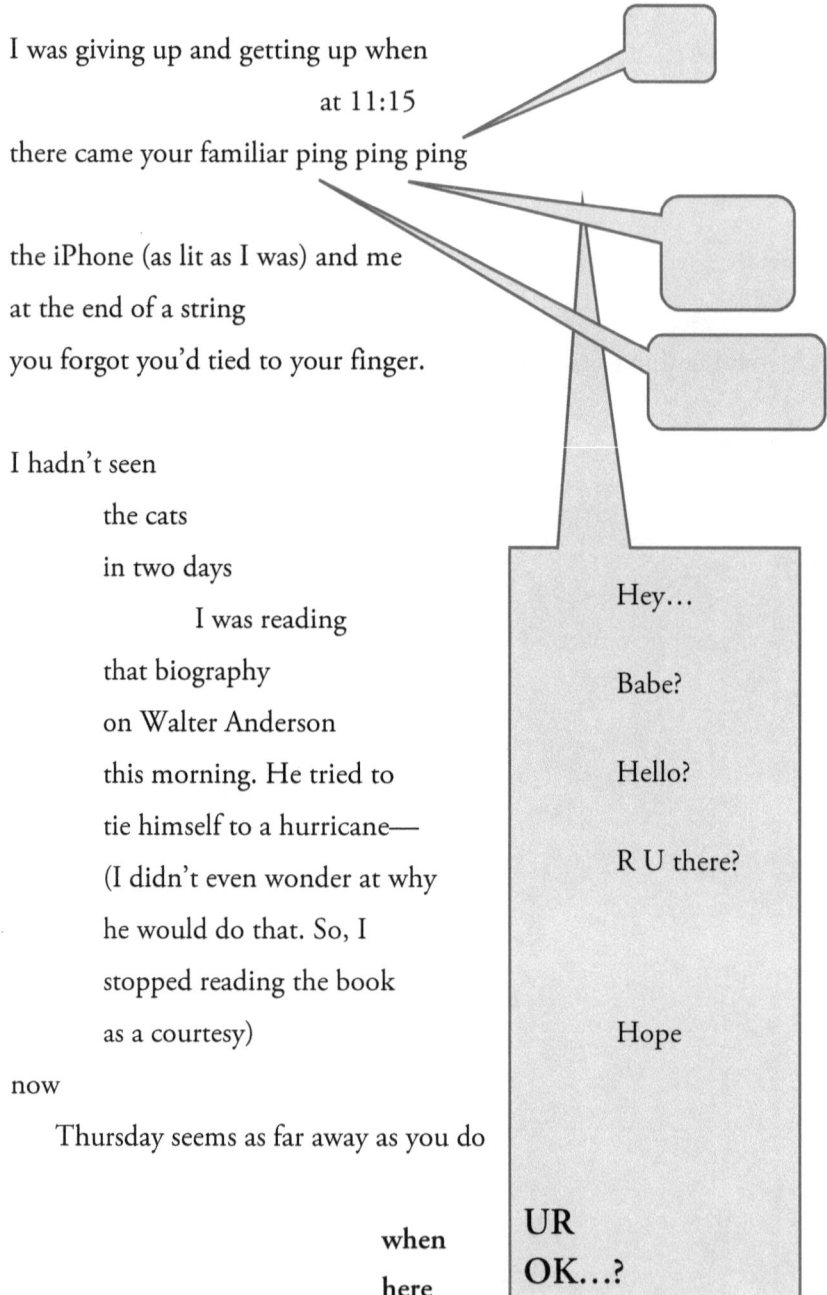

Hey…

Babe?

Hello?

R U there?

Hope

**UR
OK…?**

TRESPASS[5]

The story begins:
"They were not in love."   /   They were not that kind

of story—the good ones are written only once. They were written
to be rewritten. They kept getting misspelled, left in behind the line
    (But it is with sentence
the story begins):
    "They were whole and lovely men."
        (Or, a couple of clever stand-ins.
They didn't mind).
Isn't that the tragedy? People say. People say, *That's just the way it goes.*
(No. That's just the way it <u>starts</u>. The way it goes, that's <u>comedy).</u> / H<u>ere</u>
are two sufficient and nice men,
neck-tied to a thousand mosquitoes,
they couldn't see to count how many Canada geese, how many deer
acred in the way-back, where some evenings would appear
incredibly too soon to greedily close
out the remainder of a good day, they 'd change the subject, sitting near
as they could to each other's quiet, each in his own private gloaming.

It was in *that* moment
where the one in the glasses recalled the barbed wire tear to his shirt,

---

[5] With thanks, to JWB.

where he'd been rambling on about *Donne's "My Last Duchess,"* and had
     told
the one with the backpack that he hadn't been hurt —
(it was dulled, the barbed wire) and then, how he'd said, *No, Keats—hold
on — wrote "My Last Duchess,"* and how after that, he'd said, then,
Browning! God. Browning. Not Keats, not Donne.   /   It was *that*
     moment when

the story begins: "These two clean and decent men had had enough."
Perhaps they saw in each other too much of what could be
better, kept hidden: That dumbshow of one wasting time to be the
     Lover; one, to be in Love.
But it was dark and hard to see
                    that
               cruelty is the oldest Truth
the story begins with: One man staring at another man's back.
Both politic to the finest point, both stumps, both stiff-necked as a root
hewn into the front-door shape of someone else's home
               with dog at heel and bone.
He stares but this time he stares back. (He knows that he knows).
                    No story has two heroes.

POSTMODERN REALISM

     Here's what we know so far:
That same punishing quiet came, well-rehearsed,
with the same cue of *too dry/no flavor/undercooked*, a start
toward the same warmed-over punchline, made worse
beneath that fist (full of Man, but not Manners): So, there goes the
     plate!
         —But *the dishes do get put away, yes.*
                       Checkmate.
You've gotten very good about not leaving a mess.
Your trick is to treat a handshake like a handcuff.
You keep the curtains pulled—*next door, they could've seen us!*
   (I tell you my dream where the curtains rip apart having had enough
of me trying to keep the peace—or the table!—between us).
  You don't listen. You settle in after the second plate
     like clockwork, which always reminds me: First, Judas *ate.*

THE ONE WITH THE DAISIES

He came in
that morning
to the dining room,
full of bite, he
straddled his teeth
       and lay in wait
          while I finished

arranging the daisies—   common strays, seven
                                    average
                        common stray daisies
                        that chose our yard
                                  / we had
                        these two blue milk glass vases
                        his mother gave us
I can't remember why, I can't remember when
       for Christmas one year maybe—
       or my belated birthday—
point is, I liked these vases.
I was placing the stray daisies
in one of these vases
at the dining room table

                        his breathing made
                        the lip in the vase too narrow

                                        the way
                                        he stood toe
                                                to tooth over me.
His eyes, too. He was always able to
do that
with his eyes—
        but his hands, they were stretched open,
            each finger a bullet.   Point
                                        is, he thought it
                                        ugly, an inconsiderate waste

to make a display
of a common daisy,
in one of those vases.

                                        It's little things. You forget
to look at how little things   get underfoot, to go back for
those small words you let
hide in baby steps
            that still rub loose enough the sisal from the kitchen
            doormat,
            and once loose enough, you worry you would
            roll them into
            a hopeful rope.

                            This isn't the most flattering picture
                            of myself   I realize.

I kept thinking how fortunate I was

        to have gained weight,
        this weight.   How it gave my face more give
        under his hands.
                It made my neck take
                longer to find

      under his hands.

   I was pressed by his thighs
into the tuft of the rug
     my grandmother kidded
was her baby blanket,
    a rug that
for all its handmade love
its homemade folklore
                could not
                hold
me safe
above the hard wood floor
                could not
                hold
the hard wood floor
                back /

on my back
I kept <u>thinking</u>:
    He hates any kind of mess.
I kept <u>thinking:</u>
    Thank god

for my thighs, each thief-thick
for my neck, of Jericho-folds.
  Maybe they'd take his full focus.
  Maybe he wouldn't notice
the joke's on him—he's making
    it worse, making
      a much bigger mess—
          He doesn't realize it yet.

Because of how he shook me down into the rug which begat
how the rug shook up into the table legs   which begat
how the table upset the vase   which is how

one by one, each daisy fell
letting go
  of its petals
    petals that separated clean off the stems—
    petals that made an effort toward the foyer—
      but not in as quite
      a hurry as
      the time before, I corrected myself.

Those petals, then, each one of them!,
had gone straight
to the door—every single one!—
like they knew what it was
doors do
  I pretended
    they were scattered

        feathers torn
        from the back of a legless bird
   being made
        to walk
I pretended
        they would pull back
        together again
        this time into a single pair
        of wings
   being made
        for me—
                but no

to be fair
they weren't daisies then.
Those had been impatiens.
    Which don't do any better in vases
    than do daisies.

I made note
        of how
most of the petals fell right on the rug, like you'd expect—
I wasn't at all surprised either
that the vase acted like the floor
    was no different
    than the table.

He began crying questions. All I could comment on were the daisies.
He began shouting questions. All I could comment on were the vases.

He began to ask questions. I told him he was running late.
                                                    Then,
                                                I asked him

if he appreciated how fat
I had gotten.
Good fat, too,
free from lumps,
flush and even

as smooth
as a
baby's
bottom.

BREAK(FAST)

An ugly miracle: How Thursday was Good Night. Friday, Goodbye.
I kept that French press, not quite half-full, cooling on the table
even after you didn't reach, comfortably, for a refill. I
waited — the lamp went out then — and I thought, *Am I able
to do this...are we.* I looked up as you backed into my car, left
a dent deep and wide enough that I could see it from the kitchen door.
I'd wanted a French press. Our first Christmas. I kept
it to complete the picture of me with someone to cook breakfast for.
I watched you drive away. I was still at the door when Saturday came.
Sunday. Monday. Standing. Thinking. Far longer than I thought I was
capable of standing. (Thinking: Odd, how far *human* is from *humane*).

Thinking: I should dump out what was left of the coffee onto the table.
So I did. A grip on that French press, until my hand started to cramp.

        Then...I went after the lamp.

ALTRUISM

Jesus Christ, they were eager, bringing me empty boxes, so many
boxes from Amazon, Kroger, Wal-Mart. A few from the liquor store.
Good people, I thought. And I was thankful for that, for any
box. I said *Thank you for these boxes*. Instead: They brought more.
Those good people with their boxes. (Not once did I raise my voice,
despite the implication that they'd *done enough already, yes*).
No. I'd been *burdened in the worst way*, they said. Adding, *Not by choice!*
Asking: *Not by choice?* After awhile, it felt less a particular kindness,
more like blame, eyes cutting down what the smiles held in place,
while the whole house kept moving, a box at a time, until it was out of
the way, until there was nothing left but me standing (about-face
to boxes of chi-chis and tchotchkes convincing me I'd been loved)
captive to a surfeit courtesy of cardboard, a gesture almost as tacky
as knowing that they were really only there to stare at me.

SCAPEGOAT

1. "To Put Into Words"

we ~~make do~~
~~(we make   do? No)~~
~~(maybe?)~~
~~we~~   mean
                                    well

           (we do) but

                ~~. This is   it. This is~~
~~it.~~
we

~~make nice   necessary)~~

~~we~~   do not
                        mean
              ~~we are nice~~
~~we do not~~
           ~~mean~~   we are

                        necessary —

             ~~we mean we~~

~~ape along / we are only one because of~~

              ~~the other~~

              ~~as if~~

                        we matter

~~only~~

~~because~~

~~we will be~~

   ~~only~~

                        ~~because~~

~~we can be~~   / . . . ~~we matter~~

only

    because

        we are

within arm's reach

(you never

waved

first; so

you never

waved)

                    what isn't within
arm's reach! the entire world
is
within arm's reach
      if you walk
long
far
slow
     enough
       to

2. "Let Loose in the Wilderness"

we got
as far as town —

        we found
         neighbor with neighbor
arm in arm
  reaching
without
  making effort
unlike
us\

in the surprise wet
of that Monday night
breaking December
bread, crumbed
           into a Christmas parade
           of pageanted necks to faces
from the fatback of a borrowed pick-up truck
to the rigored bone of a tractor ankle
waving   everywhere   up
waving   everything   down

           the street full: children
were where children went
in their hurry of hurries
to yell their yells
to scream their screams[6]

(you   /didn't move
a muscle — worn down without
      /worry)

---

[6] Is this me? Did I say this?

homemade floaters throwing
half-cracked peppermint
at
the by-sitters
at
the off-lookers
all thin-eyed
all wide-lipped
    at
what was already there
(bank, courthouse, post office, church)
as if this was the first
(bank, courthouse, post office, church)
they'd ever seen
as if they had never
even *seen* before
    all thin-lipped
    all wide-eyed
at what had always been there
    way before them, back then,
    but they were here now, see?,
waiting – ready – available
      in front
          of the bank
          across from

        the courthouse
        right on the corner
        of the post office
        next to the church
    beside
   the yous and thems
   and hims and hers
      madding the crowd
into (out)liars —
each bedded to the same
bad habit of hiding
their grocery-store grief
     in public, plain-sight wholesale,
mea culpa out loud
                not bothered by ~~and despite~~ the fact
that this will not lack
the luster of the glad fool who suffers
more—each one has! and proud!—
     they have
       yet
to learn that
     the great disaster
isn't in giving the apology;
it's in accepting it;

~~(I had forgotten that~~
——————— ~~there'd be a parade)~~

it's not in
forgiving—it's in being
forgiven.

(that's why I don't wave)
no—

3. ~~"If Made to Bear the Blame"~~

~~we will not~~

———————————————~~appreciate~~
———— ~~that had we taken the time instead~~
~~to see with our ears, or~~
~~to hear with our eyes~~
——————————— ~~what was said~~
~~meant bringing fault~~
~~into full light~~
~~just not your own /~~
  ~~meant what your shoulder~~
  ~~couldn't carry~~

~~mine would.~~

~~and not ask why~~

4. "A Thing Whose Time Has Come"

because pressed coconut water
is for sale for $5.00
in West Point, Mississippi

    because it is pressed coconut water
    because it is for sale
    because it is $5.00
    because it is West Point, Mississippi

    is why

(you find $5.00
ridiculous
for water)
    I try to

turn away to
not be seen—
    as
        the fault of the small

        town is that
everybody looks
the same
direction as
everybody else
then stops—
              that is how
a round world goes flat
          and   that is how
        it stays flat
I wish you could see that
            when you slapped my mouth
            when you yelled back, "We do not!"
            when I agreed with you—
it was because sometimes
you kept your eyes
shut.

5. "— ——— ——."

            but then
        I started to think

        what
  if

I turn away
to <u>be</u> seen —
      to beg my own
           north

          south   or

                            east   west

to pretend I mattered more
to take to
      where I stood watching
and participate

            but
instead I made myself
imagine a parade
where
they threw ~~you~~

      a stone
      you missed

no

        threw you

    stone<u>s</u>

   and you missed

        them each

        and you didn't pick them each

right

back

up

        that is when I'd ask you why

(and you'd say

   Missed stones make a road, too…)

~~you would~~

~~say that,~~

   wouldn't you?

6. "The Danger of a Little Knowledge"

because
where once stood a house,— or, no, look!,
I'll say it! — a Home

has fallen
   spoiling the stitch at
   the brick,

    staining the want of

    second-hand-me-down clothes,

    stuttering the seam in

    a quiet fence

    settling old scores on

    its picnic dirt

how
the Home was
every bit its worth
of it
        held,
hostaged
by
the spreading tallow
of a
weak-long week
        smeared
across even the stock victories
          begging a myth:
    if it's
a cup of brought coffee
    if it's
the borrowed heating pad
    if it's

the noise
of you snoring
again against
the noise
of the dishwasher —
                      if it's
the truth you wanted
(you didn't but)

                      what
that did, no
does, see?,
      now?, is
it makes
work where
work doesn't belong —

in a bedroom, but
also at a kitchen table, but
      also in *our* bedroom,
      also at *our* kitchen table

it makes
work   a habit even
                      out of habit

                        of having
to remind yourself to be
still,

                        to have nothing
                        to do

with us,
it makes work

                        for me
out of loving you

and it is foreseeable
and it is a problem
and it is much
wider than the press of a place
        like West Point, Mississippi
or the shock
of five dollar water —
                        that is no threat
                                at the door —

7. "A Ghost at Feast"

— what's more
   is further
down

the road,
the few cars there
               are

have stopped, making room— /

               this Christmas
                 parade   all the floats /

after
lining up
bragging as they must /
     necessarily shrouding
as they must /
swaddled in the colors of
the gossip of Christ

   I saw you standing by
the church steps

idled and upset
at the high school
band marching past —
> (even your khakis looked
> bothered)

I wondered
at who ~~you thought~~
you were, in that particular moment,
so put out
by the crowd, the noise, the very idea
> of such!—
>> as you seemed
>>> when

we both knew you
to be a man who'd
expect
pressed coconut water
> if all he had were
> four dollars
in his pocket
>> then

you saw me seeing
you
> caught me watching

a whole round minute
we were the full display
    through the clarinets, the saxophones one minute
                two minutes
(you had your hands in gloves)

       three minutes
    as we slipped between the trumpets and trombones
            four minutes
(I had my hands in pockets)

            five minutes passed
            six minutes of us

in such
detailed noise on
full display

(you in gloves; me in pockets)
    and
that's exactly how
we stayed.

EPILOGUE

Tear off the mask
your face is
glorious
—RUMI

SAPELO

i know a good one:
josephine

up at daybruk
she said waiting

on the dock
waiting on
people

(people's people
she said)
who talk too long
about prices
about costs
about the heat
july october
january may
she said

those the people
step over sand dollars,
to pick up leftover
char from fireworks
the night before

the year before

she said
they don't know
the difference
ain't never for sale
she said

as her toe chipped a tooth,
lost,
of a bull shark,
she said
hundreds teeth

hundreds sizes
end to end bent in
the concrete shore,
an old man's jaw,
set

she said
she's boiling us shrimps
(the fire's took the grill)
she said
they gold shrimps too
(she closes the grill
with a found twig)
got for free off her
brother's daylean boat

(the good boat)

she said
the last ferry left
loud with gone-people
finning that lesser water
in doboy sound
behind us, now
behind the crown
of saw palmetto,
behind the moon,
where you couldn't see
the dock, you couldn't

see the loggerheads,
she said
the fiddle-crabs come out
she said
to play their one-arm music
she said
to wake the middlenight
she said
so the thunder can start
(at that cloud coming)
she said
so the thunder can stop
(at that cloud going)
she said

against the driftwood
she would, in a moment,
lean far enough over—
her onyx midriff large,
curves of deep lines
trenched for miles
of a lived-in back,
of squatted shoulders
that circle and circle
her, a familiar shape
of a story, of an old-time
religion, sanded down
by years of looking
at things leaving,
at loose children
tied to the always-wind

with a casual gratitude
she pulls
the bull shark tooth
free,

she said
the hard marsh sea-soil
we standing so proud on
is the oldest liar left
on this island
(next to her
uncle joe)

this hard marsh here
she said
still a bachelor
in a sweetgrass bed,
sheets sewn with secrets
of orphan teeth, whelk

she said
we made a new word
for this coast-spur
she said
'harsh' g'on, call it
'harsh' way out loud,
that's what it is,
what it's done
to us,

she said
the bull shark tooth
had come so clean
away, it lay there
in her geechee palm

suddenly

josephine flung
the bull shark tooth
far back into

the coal-ocean
where it had come from
she said
where it belongs, but don't
know what's good
for it
she said

a small child
stole away by us
his bare feet dragging
a new tide behind him,
holding a roman candle
(bullseye of light)
his child's plate laugh,
full and raw,

he made a display
of that roman candle
like we were worth it,

like
we were all worth
the bright,

brief magic
even a roman candle
can have, treading
in the shallow ribbuh

of vagabond colors,
each splitting
the quiet ink of night
into, and in threes,
for
one brief, fresh
handful of minutes
we were a whole
same kind of
magic

spoiled
by the lit fuse
burning
burned
burnt

before i could help
myself, i found
myself clapping,
at the child,
at the roman candle,
at how josephine'd worked
the fire, the grill
took the gold from the shrimp,
at all of sapelo

yes and
at her

she said
yes and

it was all good
it was all enough
i clapped
at how she knew
what was good enough

because good enough
she said
works well enough
she said

she'd come up
with a joke
(about her uncle joe
his dirty mouth,
a mynah bird and
something else
to do with the bull
shark tooth)

i didn't have time
to laugh before
she asked me

if it was funny
what did i think
she said

and
i said
it was
a good one,
josephine

About the Author

T.K. LEE is an award-winning member of the Dramatists Guild of America, the Society for Stage Directors and Choreographers, and the Association of Writers and Writing Programs, among others. In addition to poetry and drama, he has also crafted prize-winning short fiction and is core faculty in the nationally ranked MFA programs in Creative Writing as well as in Theatre Education, both at the historic Mississippi University for Women, the nation's first public academic institution for women, in Columbus, Mississippi.

About the Press

Unsolicited Press based out of Portland, Oregon and focuses on the works of the unsung and underrepresented. As a womxn-owned, all-volunteer small publisher that doesn't worry about profits as much as championing exceptional literature, we have the privilege of partnering with authors skirting the fringes of the lit world. We've worked with emerging and award-winning authors such as Shann Ray, Amy Shimshon-Santo, Brook Bhagat, Kris Amos, and John W. Bateman.

Learn more at unsolicitedpress.com. Find us on twitter and instagram.

www.ingramcontent.com/pod-product-compliance
Lightning Source LLC
LaVergne TN
LVHW040107080526
838202LV00045B/3815